José Acquelin

Anarchy of Light

Translated by Howard Scott

BookLand press

Published by BookLand Press
15 Allstate Parkway, Suite 600, Markham, Ontario L3R 5B4
www.booklandpress.com

Printed in Canada

Library and Archives Canada Cataloguing in Publication

Acquelin, José, 1956-
[Anarchie de la lumière. English]
Anarchy of light / José Acquelin; Howard Scott, translator.

Translation of: Anarchie de la lumière.
Poems.
Issued in print and electronic formats.
ISBN 978-1-77231-032-0 (paperback).--ISBN 978-1-77231-033-7 (epub).--
ISBN 978-1-77231-034-4 (pdf)

I. Scott, Howard, 1952-, translator II. Title. III. Anarchie de la lumière. English

PS8551.C68A6313 2016 C841'.54 C2016-900760-X
C2016-900761-8

Canada Council for the Arts Conseil des arts du Canada

ONTARIO ARTS COUNCIL
CONSEIL DES ARTS DE L'ONTARIO
an Ontario government agency
un organisme du gouvernement de l'Ontario

We acknowledge the financial support of the Government of Canada through the National Translation Program for Book Publishing, an initiative of the *Roadmap for Canada's Official Languages 2013-2018: Education, Immigration, Communities*, for our translation activities. We acknowledge the support of the Canada Council for the Arts, which last year invested $153 million to bring the arts to Canadians throughout the country. We acknowledge the support of the Ontario Arts Council (OAC), an agency of the Government of Ontario.

La luz es el primer
animal visible
de lo invisible

[Light is the first
visible animal
of the invisible]

~ José Lezama Lima
Quoted in the film *Our Music* by Jean-Luc Godard

Table of Contents

The Anarchist Dragonfly

What is a soul?
It is a sensibility that derives its existence
from what it is not.

~ Jean Bédard

How do I live from poetry? Not with money, that's for sure, but through the joy of a few carefree moments. Because I identify so rarely with cultural institutions – meaning those that have to be financially viable – I'll always look elsewhere if I can't see myself in them.

There are those who'll tell me that I am not avoiding the common need for narcissism by seeking to flush out the slightest hint that will pander to my insignificance. Others will call me an incurable romantic, allergic to everything that it is too directly connected with money. But really, I don't think money is dirty, it's just not really important when it comes to what I feel I need to live.

And besides, I know the denigrators well. They are above all envious of what eludes them because, basically, they can't escape their own insecurity. I'd just like them to let up a little on the reins, the muzzle or the yoke.

Habit judges swiftly, while risk tries to get out of the ruts, even if that can mean going off track or off course. But who is really lost? What I mean is who can completely go wrong in allowing oneself to discover through the otherwise, in giving oneself up from time to time to the delusions of time and the delousing of self?

I learn more from what I don't know than from what I believe or believe I know. The riches of the period accorded to us make us conscious of the time we waste. When it comes to poverty, I've known worse, including the poverty that does not have the inner means to take from it, rather than personal gain, a chance for opening, the opportunity for an alternative path.

The one who was what he never imagined he could be is no longer intent on what he would like to be. Being is not only achieved in the becoming of what you would like to be, but much more astonishingly by the coming of what you thought inconceivable. Human beings are tailored by what is beyond them and detailed by what they lack. Not everything is given to the individual or to the person, and certain things are revealed only through unexpected, unspeculative attention to certain details that point at us or penetrate us. Some speak here, and rightly so, of *serendipity*.

We cannot predict ourselves in the sights of things we advance among or in the hands of events that arise. We try to make do with, but we discover ourselves above all once unmasked, deplumed of our near-certainties. We have death insurance and we pay for it with our unpresence.

Smiles annuated, tears dehydrated, the rotting elucidated, the dying out substantiated by the weakness that nevertheless had proposed us this: to define oneself is to leave the finite behind, it is therefore to be able to take a step into the movement of infinitizing.

This is how I end up sitting among the stones on the bank of a given pond, facing the water lilies, mallards and red-winged blackbirds, when a funny kind of dragonfly sets down beside me. It has a completely white proboscis and, instead of four delicately membraned, translucent wings, four rectangular black wings.

I couldn't say if it's really a dragonfly but, for the time being, let's call it a quadruply anarchistic standard bearer. There are phenomena that you cannot calculate or fit into a given order, because those phenomena elude the common usage of numbers and words. However, some of them may turn out to be numbered. For the moment, there are four: the anarchy of the unpredictable, the anarchy of coincidence, the anarchy of beauty and the anarchy of light. Yes, truly, the mad dash of men will never catch up with the undifferentiated walk of the world.

Three Enigmas of the Heron

the more you're many
the less you're universal

if I were more alone
would I be
freer?

The eyes are always the quickest way to go to heaven. This impetus is innate. But it is still obvious that it can be more and more reckless to stick your head up. So many lassos pull us downwards, towards the screens, towards where you have to plant your feet and point them. This world is lacking heads in the clouds.

A breeze or a draft of air – does it know where it comes from and where it's going? Here and there, neither more or less. We are streams of being, no matter how slight, no matter how huge. If we do not let ourselves be devoured by devastating learning. So we desert. Let us smile at the falseness of the accountable nothings that put ire in your eyes. We should set fire to one-ways, there are no compulsory directions. Death solicits an intimate tensing you have to break away from.

In it, we burn unemptiably, we waste the freedom of no longer seeking to be. For those who can no longer tolerate going where the others would like to lead us, there is only one essence: gratuitousness, as unjustifiable as it is unbuyable in the eyes of the plutocrats.

Irrevocably, I refuse to let birth be a lifetime mortgage on death. This *eye* is not the one you think, the one I seek to make you believe in, often to be pleasant to you or sometimes to shock you. Inalienable is my inanity, each true poem proves it by uncovering confinement, by discovering a that-here, without equal, wider, without comparison with other places or instants.

A tree gratifies me with leaves on which I cannot write. No sacrifice in this regard, except an availability for no longer questioning or answering.

That is the action of the world that requires no reaction. This is the world I'm talking about and not the one that is shouting out there.

The poem is not a remix of playful sounds, not a snatching of novel images: down with the tyranny of the spectacular, with the despotism of the sensational. The poem is the gift that rescues us from the organized despoilments of every society. It unlocks wear and tear, it ruins rot, it shatters false identities. The farther it goes, the more I assent to the unidentifiable.

I walk in the warm light, the usual brain is atomized, I set down my pen butt. The settling begins.

The water lily blooms in the sun pond.

The noises do not speak the language, the language of the silencing of nature. Among the chirping of the crickets, among the rays of the epic body, among the deconstructions of humans, among the clickings of the pressurizing timer, among the rustlings of taller grasses than us, among the directed soliloquies of a mockingbird, among the sky streaks of airplanes. It is a progression among all those things and many others.

It is not progress. Except the one that goes from the self to the other, either an urban duck smoothing its feathers, an arrowhead plant with feet in the water, a flint that cannot be rubbed against forgetting.

Each hemerocallis or Philadelphia fleabane in the light of day becomes flower works - I mean a natural fire - in the middle of the flower beds of the last garden, simultaneously first and primal. Because it rises, aiming at the azure from its soil. Each flowering flower opens its eye drawn upward.

And the official heron of this notebook gravely tilts its head in the same direction, opens its beak before chirping and throwing another enigma to the goldfinches whose bodies are more yellow than the sunflowers they peck at to their heart's content:

why are your wings so black
if it is not from having learned at night
to fly

The fruit of ignorance is full of its hospitable vacuity. In munching it, we have nothing to fear since it has already swallowed us and will disgorge us shortly. Since sight has devoured us, vision will vomit our distracted gazes.

Meditations of a Silenced Minority

After a hot spring and summer, already chilly autumn. That was repeated several times: the street cannot be reserved only for cars and the sky only for spy copters. The silenced majority has been given permission to express itself. But which images, among the thousands that have been abundantly delivered to us, can remain in us as carriers of reflection on the fringes of the street? The image is a medium that approximates appearance: it's not because we receive it that we see it and understand it.

Any revolution is first of all the consequence of a certain epoch and is infused with the air of a time. Those that claim it self-proclaim with *revolutionary* reason, they consider themselves the sinews of the refusal of the state of things. Well, there is a first revolution that consists of being born of oneself, i.e. being *revolutionized*. We are not only children gnawed by the incinerator of time and the grinders of society.

Goethe said: "For all must into Nothing fall / If it will persist in Being." We should start from there. The ego of life is so huge that it impersonalizes every being that believes it says *I*. Because the multitude always favours instinct at the expense of solitude, and solitude advocates intuition. Multitude: the social overflowing the individual; solitude: the individual who cannot accept being swindled by the surroundings. While nature wanted me to be there, society, on the other hand, has very rarely convinced me of the necessity of my life. The sole necessity of life appears to me in the burgeoning consciousness of my death, which gives birth to the freedom of my solitude through the obvious solitude of my freedom. But what can that which I claim to be the freedom of my solitude do against the reality advocated by the potentates of the concrete?

It is perfectly human to not know how to live well. It is often even considered normal that you have to eat your dark bread before the white morsel of your marvels. I no longer believe in this standard of sorrow before the sweetness of merit, even if it remains true that we don't see how to escape the instant of pain when it strikes. But now the sky is sobering up. The light gives an ocular breeze to those who, starting at dusk, work to the gleam of a pen to light up the starry night, which will never be total inky darkness. So let us come out of the earth, walk, perpendicular to the horizon: the stars are winged diamonds that the sleepers know nothing of.

Whatever the deepest woods, the most remote regions – where there is no human to hear anything at all – the closest alley, the most concreted of suburbs or the most immediate and banal scenery where you can find yourself, do you know a bird that, at the hour when the light breaks, will refrain from singing? In what, for what or for whom should the humans feel obligated to act differently? In the name of which superiority? Superiority of conscience? What do we think we understand more than a blackbird? Each new day is a new youth of the world.

Hoist your baseness to the heights of land, don't squeeze the lump of your heart. Through the half-open door, the smell of the earth stirred up gives gardeners back the courage of lungs. The air duct in itself offers heaven and the self two spontaneous motivations to effortlessly forsake current events. Is there elevation in education? Man descends from the monkey and the monkey goes back up to the oldest tree of the world to get close to the arms of the sun. Even at night, you find the sky beautiful: first and last proof of our idealism, which, however, really doesn't know what to do with our down-to-earthism. But never have the sky and earth been completely in conflict, or else we wouldn't be here to hope or despair. Yes, too often the full light of day blinds us to the constellations of our cerebral oyster.

Each has their secret universes that are not necessarily unmentionable, but that turn out to be and often will turn out to be inadmissible, especially by individuals of power and control or the media, who decide what is acceptable or what is not. The sense of freedom of some will always clash with the clichés of obedience of others. Equality opposes nothing. Because it does not exist. Because it is. Equality of being able to live even though we are not all alike.

Useless like all idealists, I barely speak, I speak against a pain that is not only mine. And I write for the pain, which is beyond me. To take care of a fire means watching that the flame is not smothered in smoke.

Collateral Liberties

All your life you search for the place of origin, the place from before the world, that is, the place where the ego can be absent and where the body is forgotten.

~ Pascal Quignard

Each goes toward their little freedoms among obligations and commitments. Simple solitudes between self and self that have nothing to do with egocentric individualism, but with instants when you feel the very legitimate need to filter the external imperatives, the circumstantial jostlings, the uncontrollable unexpected.

Decant, unbind, peel yourself, call yourself outside your name. Do nothing in particular, get out from between your two ears, even if you have to open up a third to true silence. We can't talk about a final rejection of the world, but about a shortage in our private universe, about a necessary recourse to a vital void. Unstick ourselves from the images affixed to us, including those we've used in order to function, but that have planed us down. Extricate ourselves from the common stream, save for ourselves a low tide to gape or gripe solitarily.

Because it must be repeated that our path across the social slaughterhouses offers no permanent guarantee of being able to avoid them. Recognizing yourself as a lost lamb, without falling into self-satisfaction, has a certain advantage since you grant yourself the right to escape past or present blamings. Perhaps we could even recognize the need for a feeling of naïveté and innocence, or a nostalgia for the carefree days of our childhood with, in the bargain, a possible conciliation with the time that remains for us as consenting extras, with clear and affable faces.

> *Much has been said about one famous man who walked on the water, but very little about the insect water walkers, the water beetles called* whirligigs *that make circles on water surfaces. What is considered a miracle for one constitutes the ordinary for others. Moving over the crystalline lens of a pond or a lake limpidly reflecting the sky is therefore not only the prerogative of Christ.*

To meditate is first of all to observe the mirror of the universe, its perceptible reflection. Meditation facilitates the sifting out of many hackneyed beliefs. But 99.99 % of the time we are in a belief, in order to be able to tolerate the temporality to be crossed - no time is continuously easy. Having one faith or another, profane or sacred, superstitious or rationalist, is a crutch to use in hopes of one day walking better. And we never stop learning to walk. Because meditating means being able to stop wanting to move forward and no longer desiring to understand, explain, swagger. You don't settle down, you sit down, in a trifle where you can no longer even believe in yourself. Time is the greatest illusionist there is: there is nothing but being. To meditate is to purify the light of our blindness.

> *In the kingdom of the squirrels there are only oaks. In the middle of the nothing shed by history, by our story, there remains only our ganders on the grandeur of the equalization of all fates.*

Then, in the face of the sole visible eye of the day that cuts right through us, there is no more rampart to protect us from our naïveté. The human artifice burns, words slip away from themselves, one goes quiet, knows oneself free to know everything. The science of being begins here, in that unlocatable *there,* in the consciousness of the first and ultimate dispossession: the science of being introduces you to the consciousness of not being.

It is like a calming tenderness that you prescribe for yourself, a private oasis, the learning of our erasure, a kind of serenity outside of the rink and the rings, an end already in the self and from the self with no means other than what remains of natural beauties.

It is a tiny peace full of the waves of our breathing, a tranquility that summons us to a tender extinction of things and beings.

It is a tame end of what we called our lives, all the regrets or remorse dissipated.

It is the exile from our narrowness where we would cleanse ourselves of our obsession with looking good in order to, finally, be free of ourselves.

And it is only justness rendered to the nudity that transfigures us.

Verses from the Orphanage of the World

No echo is lost, not even the silence of before the universe.

✣

Inexplicably there are still poets, these omega beings, nearly the only ones to provide unpredictable answers to common questions. With, conversely, the philosophers, who ask insoluble questions in the face of ready-made answers. The main reason being that the two of them cohabit in the same humiliated humility called humanity.

✣

Deceitfully I tell you: to better leave, it is very human and easier to hate the world rather than to wait for the sigh of joy it will give at our end.

✣

The silence is so unheard-of that it has never been anything but the degree zero of everything starting with which nothing is infinitely possible.

Music, the music that disposes of language, and therefore clothes, builds a bridge, the only one capable of no longer seeking to translate the silence verbosely, where there is now neither a preworld nor a postworld.

In all ways, however realistic or scientific, this world does not exist, can no longer excite except in the hallucination of believing in the susceptibility of our senses. Because to be born is to provoke the origin that knows nothing of its purpose.

Already it is smoking us by lighting the paper of our skin around the tobacco of our bones, freedom has always done without us better to scorn, at the bottom of the hourglass, the ashtray that we know we have to be but which we dress up with the word *consciousness*.

⁜

That is all we have left, love, and I don't know how to talk to you without betraying the beauty that has praised us, unconditionally, for an innocence so great that it ignored the animality that has founded and fused us. The fusion can only take place through the random confusion of a universe without choices, cyclically burning. All fire is blind but offers seeing.

⁜

Real lovers are always orphans of the world, without intentions nor gods.

⁜

And then after so many ends of the world, there is always the struggle of the elements that will never be able to quiet down to rise up, with other flames, toward a riddle more mysterious than the fossils of our love, in the heart of a meteorite.

✣

The orphanage of the world is truly the proof of the freedom of our solitude only on this condition: it unties us from it, therefore from ourselves.

✣

We really wouldn't be able to pretend: how can we not recognize the perpetual incompleteness of our ignorance?

✣

From mineral uteruses to parietal hands, from the overthrow of the first predators, from the warrior persistence in possessing more territory more and more, what keeps us from refusing to die to make way for other modes of beings, tranquil there?

✣

I take responsibility for the vanity of my voice; it is part of my inaudible privilege and my trampable tracks. But this is the way that I'm as old as those who will refuse to be born in that world. Runt's honour.

✣

Some will have me on. It is easy of push away the dying of living and laughing when we no longer feel like being born in crying and in blood. A night will come, silently perfect, which will allow those who remain to judge vagaries, without any salvageable social or linguistic distinction.

✣

Return to the metaphysics of your nest, negator of the life that received you. Perhaps you will give back to the woman who swelled the lungs of your soul the incomparable joy of believing that her suffering was not fruitless in the face of the one that is yours and with which you comfort the others in their state of blissful imbeciles.

✣

As long as I last, I will not retrace my steps, on the thoughts that convinced me to go farther in my weaknesses. I will have been able to do what I did, and it will not be better than what I could have been if I had had the means of my peasant roots.

✣

Finally, I know nothing of where I come from. But any good peasant will always be able to show you where their lands end, and recognize that beyond their fences, it is not their cultivations that are going to change their nature, the labour of their days, the seeds of their hopes and the harvest of their reality. Because from the beginning to the end, the art of transiting is not so much to demand, but just a way to maintain the claim.

✣

I can no longer flower the things that have made me object or reject. I rest from not being able to follow. Every life is so unequal, in relationship to any other, that it thus becomes unequalled. So I will soon go, at the end of these poems and this night, to lunch at the antisocial funerals of my remorse and at the velvety cremation of my regrets.

✣

But how can you bury your entire pride? As stupid and simple as this: there is no recipe to being right and knowing how to feed the pure thirst of being without end.

Compressed Hearts and Repressed Bodies

There, very softly. If necessary, don't do anything, don't wake up anyone. Each to their mirage: Sol is the soil of no foot, but the root of all eyes.

We have always known it: power corrupts. Human nature is thus overrated, especially since it was given the vertical status of a super-animal. This arrogant prerogative, from era to era, from civilization to civilization, is truly far from abating. It lays waste to its surroundings, it plunders the Earth and strips of simple everyday courage all those who ask only to be happy without feeling conned at every turn, with each law passed, with each piece of oligarchic propaganda, with each devious contortion of High Phynance. Labile alibi for the one of those who cling to their privileges through an incurable fear of losing them. Labile, faltering, because that reveals their faults. They confuse having and being, wanting and living, power and presence. What could make them change except for failure, falls, disappointment, disillusion? Sometimes, we tell ourselves that awareness of the very short human lifespan should at least convince them of the fragility of their lives and the lives of others. But no, nothing seems to be able to deliver compressed hearts from their stubbornness. Is it the atavistic instinct of predation that holds them in its talons? Do they imagine that if they don't stop devouring they will never be swallowed in their turn? Have they never suffered so they continue to cause suffering? Don't they just go dizzy with evading a pain rooted deeply within them, to better believe they would no longer have to face it? From what and from whom are they trying to escape? There is good reason to get lost in fleeting, murky conjectures while trying to understand what embeds them in the setting.

I release the compressed hearts and go visit a friend with a repressed body. He needs to talk to me. He feels tired, exhausted. He feels no longing to go elsewhere or farther away. Any more than he understands what he is, what he's doing here. What he is experiencing no longer persuades him away from a fascinating follow-up. It seems to him that any relationship with the other requires a capacity to negotiate with a suffering of which we cannot discern to what extent it is ours or the reflection of that of the other on us. In this world of debit or credit, he doesn't even want to know what he owes or what he may be owed. He can't take it anymore, whatever the transaction to be accepted or refused. He says: this world is poor of real news and a billionaire in inevitable repetitions. He feels exhausted and now has but a single desire, it is to get away from his tenuousness. Some die for less than that. He insists: me and this world? A single formless, corroded, abused entity. I am nothing but a doddery, valetudinarian ectoplasm, and I don't see what incarnation I could enlist in.

I hope for an instant to comfort him by pointing out to him that he is not lacking for words to say what he is experiencing and feeling. He replies to me that he values less and less this favour granted by his education that he likens to strict if not constrictive training. He says: the birthing does not predict the being, loving does not pay cash and dying reopens the eternal file. I say: no death certifies us that we have to go into exile from birth. He says: however, the day dies quickly if the light empties the eyes and does not open the reality of boredom to the brightness of night. I say: it is true that very often existing is like smoking without fire. Youth doesn't have the time, middle age invents questions, old age has no more answers, human duration is incontinent. He says: yes, we don't know what knows us, we don't look at what sees us, we can't have what we are, we go through doors without understanding. I say: but there comes a moment when you have to forgive your fate for having been too hard or too easy. A match has never burned the sun, jealousy serves only our truth, no poplar rejects a catbird, rain has never drowned the ocean. And beauty pities those who avoid it.

He says: that's very nice, very poetic all that, but what do you do with wear? I suggest: the art of growing old comes from what you no longer need to be. Is it possible to envisage a peace of solitude in the plainsong of silence? He says: tell me then, how does the silence deal with unsinkable desire? I say: there is no giving in to desire, this momentum, this drive of the living, there is only one desire, which does not give in to being transformed. He says: to be continued then…

The Between Worlds

I grow old, I accumulate the dead around me, I am more and more musty, less and less me.

When you leave, you have no more desire for here. Because you are already no longer there, in that dimension that you have to leave. A friend, very conscious of his impending death, said: while life can sometimes be shared among the living, death cannot be shared, even with those you love the most. There is a unification of the self, an indivisibility of one's own person, hermetic even to those closest, which perhaps means that you have never been as much yourself even when you are assured of no longer being able to be. And that scares those who remain. Life is deaf to death, blinded by what it refuses to be concerned with.

There is no greater democracy than death, but also nothing more solitary. Consequently there is no greater solitude than that of the living who refuse awareness of their future dying. Hence the utopia of democracy. I hate realists as soon as they think themselves real. They hate me back as soon as I think myself realer than them. Basically, reality is the field of the first battle that takes place only on the surface of events, over the area of the Earth. It is the dead who are right, under earth or in heaven. It matters little since they are cold to our trivial matters or else beyond them. Farther from the self you can consider things, you can no longer be yourself. And this is a good thing. If, among humans, there are things or beings that are not repeated, that permits myths to be born so that this way the terrans believe themselves exempted from dying.

In order not to have to die, it would be necessary not to be born. That is not our freedom. If there is one freedom, it is uncompromising, it is the privilege of a goddess who gets by without all the little gods that we believe we are. In this universe of matter so effective that it effaces, our papier-mâché ideas and our fleeting feelings constitute our celibate reality forever. If a truer truth remains for us, it is our sole solitude, that enclosure of our death, that may be able to save our lives.

The world of humans is so terribly precarious that it is easy to understand why they invented gods to help them tolerate themselves. Faith is no doubt only the confession of our own weaknesses thrown at everything that goes beyond our condition and our conditioning. That confession can also be called prayer. There is no prayer that has reversed the rage of existing in the hope of another age, in the desire for another time, including that elementary longing to no longer depend on any time, therefore to be dead to our miseries or to be just dead.

Sometimes it's nice weather and we rain, sometimes it cries and we shine. Sometimes we get out of the requisite law, sometimes we enter into the unsuspected. Sometimes there is no more reliable faith. This sadness of humanity that never knows what and how to do to be differently from the one self. Every day is too long, too dully endless for the infinite of a misunderstood second on the clocks. The pendulum of the heart only runs on the blood given to love so that it can try in spite of everything to go on. Who can allow themselves not to imitate the sun? But too often we burn our loved ones and we turn those who don't burn.

From the sun, life is a prison where the blackbirds sing, where the moon whitewashes and where you have to free yourselves before exiting. This is how the soul becomes a horned beetle, the heart a violet crocus, the spirit a circonvoluting buzzard, the past an ashen narcissus and the present a stellar reflection that permits us, sometimes with indulgence, to cross the night of the future. We are only there to make life live, to make death die with our naive ignorance and our gap words. We are only here to pass through the passage, pass beyond the revolt against the incomprehensible. Eternally, there is nothing to explain; simultaneously nothing to prove.

Only a breath that models, modulates and outmodes us in a game of silence and fury, in a fire of commotion and suffocation, in that little time that pushes us to invent the infinite, simply out of fear of the finished and lack of genius.

Seen from an airplane, organic reality in rounded movements, the Earth already seems more acceptable. How much more stunning when it is seen from on high. Let the sky descend in us to uproot us from our clay and lead us back toward the candour of our cosmic dusts. There is no external experience that is not related to an interior experience. The perspective given by the fact of advancing in age turns out to be that of living more and more simply and without oneself-assurance. I assent to the physical slowness to detach myself from the required social speed. I even corroborate immobility to favour a natural nomadism of the spirit. I dissociate myself more easily from my psychological struggles for a presence without dues to pay to the past or the future.

I no longer count on this or that, I count down, through the beauty of the less, to this strange ideal that is zero. Any acknowledged loss of objective goes along with an agreed annihilation of the subjective. On condition of seeing in it neither respite nor spite, it borders on primal fulfilment.

Even with my eyelids closed, I see the crimson sun. Then I imagine a book to read with closed eyes. Starting with our intimate night. With a few retinal afterimages as our only lighting. And also with this recurring question: what can we retain from this world to go through the remaining days?

Stellarium

The unthinkable is the only image that can satisfy the one who contemplates it.

~ François Jacqmin

Like any being, fragment of earth, I wait: which amounts to sectioning time, to selecting according to a plan mapped out by the need to make something or someone happen at any price. To neglect the present is to prevent it from coming through us when it permeates us prior to any will. It is less a matter of being of your time than of being of time, period. To paraphrase an Amerindian saying about the Earth: time does not belong to us, we belong to time. And, in fact, we are just one of the belongings of time, a nomad longing constantly being transformed. There is only one art, and it is the art of living. I believe that any artist works especially when the others are not working or want to rest from their jobs.

More intimately, I am convinced that any artist is fundamentally worked up by what others do not have the time to work out: time.

If there is a single speed at which I would like to go, it is the one that would permit me to maintain myself exactly under the closest star; even if it means burning still more quickly and dooming circadian rhythm to oblivion. Since that cannot be, I therefore go very slowly, always running behind the solar light.

If an orange can tinge the air with blue, can the composure of the Earth soothe the freneticals? Faced with the patient tectonic drifts of the soils where we expose and repose our toes, we are only episodic epiphenomena. The little understanding of things that you can brush with the lightning of time conceded does not seem to be able to heal us of ourselves. What wisdom can we take from our inaptitude at extricating ourselves from the manifest dimensions? The flying palmiped, which takes its nap in the shadow of the nearest larch, doesn't give a damn about the question any more than any resolution. But when the din of our movements fades, the unthinkable takes the shape of a powdered thought that you let fly away at the first abrupt breeze. If the air passes so easily, why worry about its invitation to imitate it? There are times when you say very clearly to yourself: what good is the blackness of our swarmings?

We ingest matter as much as we are digested by it. In short, we direct nothing. We are engendered as we generate. Matter is only a partial manifestation of what we believe ourselves capable of perceiving. Imagining is not a personal faculty: everything inter-reacts. It is therefore not a matter of how and why to be. That matters beyond available predictions. The poem does not negotiate with the quantifiable; it is produced by the unspeakable that it can itself bring into the worlds. We are by what is already and we invent ourselves through the deficiency of being other than what we are said to be. To disobey is to move outside the self and let yourself be drawn by what eludes us. The poem invites us to detoxify ourselves from a laboured existentialism. There is not only life and death, doing and undoing, the know-how and the urgency of being undone. There is what we cannot have - we have already been had. There is what we will know if we are deborn from the incorporated limits.

Today, there is no one in the garden. Only lost beliefs and buoyant red-winged blackbirds, dark-eyed juncos and hospitable chickadees that lead, with natural sound, my song in soan*. A fine smoke immolates the instant, time idolizes nothing. Hence its neutral glory, unattainable for those who pass by only to make of themselves an agitated fire of uncontrollable elements. While deep down as on the surface, the non-principle coincides very precisely with the non-purpose. Or, more simply, when there is no more when that holds me by the hand.

All thoughts leaning toward a general "hush!", the birds make silence and I hear the unimaginable from a motionless wind. The blue of the sky joins the green of the trees through the yellow of the sun. One day there will be no more day, one night there will be no more night. Perfect equality where the word *light* will itself have become obsolete.

* *Soan*: in Japan, a small teahouse, facing a garden or landscape, designed so you can immerse yourself in the beauty of nature.

About the Translator

Howard Scott was born in southwestern Ontario and moved to Quebec in 1975. His translation of *L'Euguélionne* by Louky Bersianik won the Governor General's Literary Award in 1997. He has translated many poetry, fiction, and non-fiction titles, often in collaboration with Phyllis Aronoff. In 2001, they won the Quebec Writers' Federation Translation Award and in 2009 they were shortlisted for the Governor General's Literary Award. He is a past president of the Literary Translators' Association of Canada. He currently lives in Montreal.